Contents

S0-AWJ-455

Special pull-out chart

Fifteen truths about Jesus

World Religions made easy

Mark Water

HENDRICKSON
PUBLISHERS

World Religions Made Easy
Hendrickson Publishers, Inc.
P.O. Box 3473
Peabody, Massachusetts 01961-3473

Photography supplied by
Digital Stock, Digital Vision,
Goodshoot, Photo Alto, Photodisc
and Tony Cantale

Illustrations by
Tony Cantale Graphics

First printing – September 1999
Reprinted – May 2002

Manufactured in China

The religions of the world

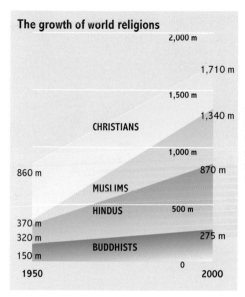

The growth of world religions

CHRISTIANS

MUSLIMS

HINDUS

BUDDHISTS

2,000 m
1,710 m
1,500 m
1,340 m
1,000 m
870 m
860 m
500 m
370 m
320 m
275 m
150 m
0

1950
2000

Islam is growing
By the year 2010 there could be more Muslims in the world than Christians.

ISN'T ONE RELIGION AS GOOD AS THE NEXT?

Is there only one way to God?
With the three major world religions all on the increase, and with the many flourishing cults, it is vital for Christians to know the answer to the question: Is Jesus the only way to God?

Jesus Christ claimed to be *the* way to God.

"I am the way and the truth and the life. No one comes to the Father except through me." JOHN 14.6

A question of truth
As you investigate other religions and cults ask yourself these questions:
- How did they originate?
- Do they agree or disagree with the teaching of the Bible?
- What do they think of God?
- Who do they think Jesus is?

What's so special about Christianity?

SOME CLAIMS OF CHRISTIANITY

Christianity makes a number of bold claims. Christians not only believe that Christianity is true, but that all other world religions cannot be compared favorably with Christianity.

When it comes to salvation Christians believe that Christ alone provides the path to God.

1. Christianity believes that Jesus is God in the flesh

Christians say: If you want to know who God is like, then look at Jesus Christ.

"He [Christ] is the image of the invisible God." COLOSSIANS 1:15

2. The crucifixion of Jesus is central to Christianity

The Protestant reformer, Martin Luther, recommended that one should look at the death of Jesus in order to find out what Christianity is all about.

"If you want to understand the Christian message you must start with the wounds of Christ."
MARTIN LUTHER

3. Christianity believes that there is hope for the individual

No religion deals with the sin problem like Christianity.

The Bible teaches that:

• Sin separates us from God.
"Your iniquities have separated you from your God." ISAIAH 59:2

• God hates sin.
"Your eyes are too pure to look on evil; you cannot tolerate wrong."
HABAKKUK 1:13

• When Jesus died on the cross he was punished instead of us, so we could receive forgiveness.
"He himself bore our sins in his body on the tree." 1 PETER 2:24

This was the only way the sin problem could be dealt with.

Christians say: If you want salvation and freedom from sin, evil and guilt, trust in Jesus for forgiveness.

"In him [Jesus] we have redemption through his blood, the forgiveness of sins, in acccordance with the riches of God's grace that he lavished on us with all wisdom and understanding." EPHESIANS 1:7-8

The cross is the symbol of Christianity.

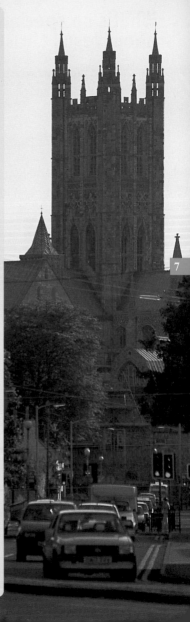

4. Christianity claims to point the way to heaven

Other religions teach that it is necessary to do something personally in order to earn the right to enter heaven – like become a better and purer person.

Christianity is unique in teaching that a person cannot do anything to win a place in heaven, but rather has to accept what Jesus Christ has done on his or her behalf.

Christianity teaches that no amount of good deeds carried out in this life, or prayers prayed on behalf of another after they have died, can help a person to gain heaven.

Christianity teaches that salvation and heaven are a gift offered to an individual by God. To receive this gift of salvation and heaven, the individual must accept the gift by faith.

"For it is by grace you have been saved, through faith – and this not from yourselves, it is the gift of God – not by works, so that no one can boast." EPHESIANS 2:8-9

What's so special about Jesus Christ?

"Christianity is Christ"
If you want to understand about Christianity it is best to start with Jesus.

How does Jesus differ from other religious teachers?

• Jesus the teacher
Jesus' most well known teaching comes in the Sermon on the Mount. See Matthew 5–7.

• Jesus taught his followers that love is an active verb.
"Love your enemies and pray for those who persecute you."
MATTHEW 5:44

"In everything, do to others what you would have them do to you."
MATTHEW 7:12

• Jesus said he was God
Jesus went much further than giving good moral advice. Jesus claimed to be God himself.

"'I tell you the truth,' Jesus answered, 'before Abraham was born, I am!'" JOHN 8:58

"I AM" was the name God used when he spoke to Moses. See Exodus 3:14. So when Jesus said, "before Abraham was born, I am!" he was claiming to be God, and was using God's name.

• Jesus acted like God
1. Jesus spoke with authority.
   "The crowds were amazed at his teaching, because he taught as one who had authority, and not as their teachers of the law."
   MATTHEW 7:28-29

9

THE BEATITUDES

Jesus started his Sermon on the Mount with the Beatitudes.

"Blessed are the poor in spirit, for theirs is the kingdom of heaven.
Blessed are those who mourn, for they will be comforted.
Blessed are the meek, for they will inherit the earth.
Blessed are those who hunger and thirst for righteousness, for they will be filled.
Blessed are the merciful, for they will be shown mercy.
Blessed are the pure in heart, for they will see God.
Blessed are the peacemakers, for they will be called sons of God.
Blessed are those who are persecuted because of righteousness, for theirs is the kingdom of heaven.
Blessed are you when people insult you, persecute you and falsely say all kinds of evil against you because of me."

MATTHEW 5:3-11

2. Jesus forgave sins.
"When Jesus saw their faith, he said, 'Friend, your sins are forgiven.'" LUKE 5:20

3. Jesus controlled the elements.
"He [Jesus] got up, rebuked the wind and said to the waves, 'Quiet! Be still!' Then the wind died down and it was completely calm." MARK 4:39

4. Jesus raised others from the dead.
"Jesus called in a loud voice, 'Lazarus, come out!' The dead man came out, his hands and feet wrapped with strips of linen, and a cloth around his face." JOHN 11:43-44

5. Jesus rose from the dead himself. See Luke 24.

What about Judaism?

Judaism

- Judaism is the oldest revealed religion.
- It is monotheistic, believing in the existence of one God.

The start of Judaism

God called one person, Abraham. God then chose Abraham's descendants to be his special people.

"The Lord had said to Abram, 'Leave your country, your people and your father's household and go to the land I will show you. I will make you into a great nation and I will bless you; I will make your name great, and you will be a blessing. I will bless those who bless you, and whoever curses you I will curse; and all peoples on earth will be blessed through you.'" GENESIS 12:1-3

Jews and worship

The people of Israel worshiped God because they believed that they had been expressly chosen by God – a special people called to be holy. Moses told the people of Israel:

"For you are a people holy to the Lord your God. The Lord your God has chosen you out of all the peoples on the face of the earth to be his people, his treasured possession." DEUTERONOMY 7.6

The Jews expressed their thanks for God's actions in their worship.

"It is good to praise the Lord and make music to your name,
    O Most High,
to proclaim your love in the
    morning
and your faithfulness at night."
PSALM 92.1-2

Jewish belief

The Jews believe that the purpose of life is summed up in love for God:

"Love the Lord your God with all your heart and with all your soul and with all your strength" DEUTERONOMY 6:5,

and love for one's neighbor:

"Love your neighbor as yourself." LEVITICUS 19:18

This love is based on the love God has for his people. The way to express love for God and one's neighbor is set out in the Ten Commandments.

THE TEN COMMANDMENTS

God gave the Ten Commandments to his special people. These are listed in full in Exodus 20:1-17, and may be summarized as follows:

1. You shall have no other gods besides me.

2. You shall not worship any idol.

3. You shall not misuse God's name.

4. Remember the Sabbath day and keep it holy.

5. Honor your father and your mother.

6. You shall not murder.

7. You shall not commit adultery.

8. You shall not steal.

9. You shall not give false testimony.

10. You shall not covet anything that belongs to your neighbor.

Key words unraveled

Decalogue
The *Decalogue* is another name for the Ten Commandments

Torah
The scrolls of the first five books of the Old Testament – Genesis, Exodus, Leviticus, Numbers, and Deuteronomy – make up the *Torah*. It is known as God's law and is also referred to as the five books of Moses.

Mishnah
The *Talmud* is a compilation of Jewish oral teaching that expands on the *Mishnah*, a collection of traditions and practices intended for individual and communal sanctification. The *Midrash* is ancient commentary on the Bible.

Synagogue
Synagogue comes from a Greek word meaning 'a gathering together.' It stands for the gathering of the dispersed (*Diaspora*) – Jews who met together for worship and study.

Additional information on Judaism

The Jewish religion is based on the Hebrew Bible (the Christian Old Testament) and oral teaching set down in the Talmud and Rabbinic tradition

Jewish traditions supplement the teachings of the Old Testament. For example, the washing of hands before and after a meal is not in the Old Testament and was not for cleaning hands, but was a ritual cleansing based on rabbinic tradition.

So the Pharisees asked Jesus, "Why do your disciples break the tradition of the elders? They don't wash their hands before they eat!"

Jesus replied with this stern rebuke: "And why do you break the command of God for the sake of your tradition? ...

You nullify the word of God for the sake of your tradition." See Matthew 15:1-7

Jews do not understand the Old Testament as prophesying about Jesus

For the Jews, the "Bible" is the Old Testament. (This was true in the times of Jesus also.) The Jews could recite many chapters from the Old Testament from memory.

But Jesus accused them of missing the most important thing about the Old Testament.

"You diligently study the Scriptures because you think that by them you possess eternal life. These are the Scriptures that testify about me, yet you refuse to come to me to have life." JOHN 5:39-40

Old Testament texts that Christians understand as prophecies about Jesus

1. His birthplace	Micah 5:1-2
2. His birth by a virgin	Isaiah 7:14
3. Rejection by his own people	Isaiah 53:3
4. Betrayal by a close friend	Psalm 41:9
5. Events as he died	Psalms 22:14-18
6. The Messiah's sacrifice for his people	Isaiah 53:6
7. His resurrection from the dead	Psalms 16:10; 49:15

The Jews do not believe that Jesus Christ is God's promised Messiah

The Jews believed, and still believe, that the Messiah (the Anointed One) will come from the nation of Israel, from the tribe of Judah, and be a descendant of David.

They have wonderful prophecies about the expected Messiah:

"For to us a child is born,
to us a son is given,
and the government shall be on his shoulders.
And he will be called
   Wonderful Counselor, Mighty God,
   Everlasting Father, Prince of Peace."
ISAIAH 9:6

But Jews do not believe John's witness to Jesus:

"Jesus is the Christ, the Son of God" (JOHN 20:31).

13

God has a plan for the Jews

Paul, a converted Jew, wrote about God's plans for the Jews in Romans 9–11.

"I do not want you to be ignorant of this mystery, brothers, so that you may not be conceited: Israel has experienced a hardening in part until the full number of the Gentiles has come in. And so all Israel will be saved." ROMANS 11:25-26

A prayer that orthodox Jews pray every day

We are your people, the children of Abraham your friend, to whom you spoke on Mount Moriah;
   the descendants of Isaac, who was bound on the altar;
   the congregation of Jacob, your firstborn son.
... It is therefore our duty to thank, praise and glorify you,
to bless, to sanctify and to offer praise and thanksgiving to your name.
Happy are we! How good is our portion, and how pleasant our lot, and how beautiful our heritage.

What about Islam?

Who are the adherents of Islam?

Their origin is dated to the prophet Muhammad who lived in the 7th century. Muslims regard Muhammad as their final prophet, but by no means their first prophet.

Facts and figures

- Islam is the fastest growing world religion.
- In 1900 there were 200,000,000 Muslims.
- In 1950 there were 370,000,000 Muslims.
- In 2000 there will be 1,340,000,000 Muslims.
- Over six million Muslims live in America.

THE FIVE PILLARS OF ISLAM

These "pillars" are obligations which faithful Muslims are expected to observe.

1.	Profession of faith	"There is no other God but God and Muhammad is his prophet."
2.	Worship	Worship is to be observed five times each day.
3.	Alms-giving	Over 2% of one's wealth is to be paid to the poor.
4.	Fasting	Fasting is to be observed during the month of Ramadan.
5.	Pilgrimage	A pilgrimage, or Hajj, is to be made to Mecca.

Key words unraveled

Islam
Islam means "submission," that is, submission to God.

Qur'an
The *Qur'an*, also known as the *Koran*, is Islam's scripture and its final authority. It was purportedly revealed to Muhammad in a series of visions.

Muezzin
A *muezzin* calls the faithful Muslims to prayer in their mosque, the Muslim public place of worship.

Mecca
The town of *Mecca* is the holy city of Islam and the center for pilgrimage.

The Islamic creed
The five main articles of the Islamic creed are:
1. Belief in one God
2. Belief in angels
3. Belief in prophets
4. Belief in revealed scripture
5. Belief in a day of judgment

An Islamic prayer
In the name of the One God,
    the Compassionate One,
    the Merciful.
Praise be to God, the Lord of the
    Universe –
The Compassionate One, the
    Merciful –
The Ruler on the Day of Judgment.
We worship you and from you we
    seek help.
Guide us into the straight path –
The path of those to whom you
    have shown mercy –
Not those who have incurred your
    anger, nor those who go astray.

FROM THE BEGINNING OF THE QUR'AN, KNOWN AS 'THE OPENING.' A DEVOUT MUSLIM REPEATS THIS PRAYER FIVE TIMES A DAY.

Muhammad and his sin
Unlike Christ who was sinless, Muhammad claimed that God said to him: "I have taken away your sins that have bent your back."

Additional information on Islam

Belief about God

There is a basic difference between the teaching of the Bible and the teaching of the *Qur'an* about the character of God.

Some Islamic teachers say that there are 99 names for God in the *Qur'an*. However, "God is love" is not one of them. Muslims believe that God is too high and mighty to relate to mere humans. Even in paradise Muslims do not expect to discover that God is a God of love.

Allah expects us to love him before he loves us. "Say, (O Muhammad, to mankind); If you love Allah, follow me; Allah will love you." "If ye love Allah ... Allah will love you." QUR'AN 2:195; 3:31

But the apostle John wrote: "This is how God showed his love among us: He sent his one and only Son into the world that we might live through him. This is love: not that we loved God, but that he loved us and sent his Son as an atoning sacrifice for our sins." 1 JOHN 4:9-10

Belief about Jesus

Jesus is mentioned 97 times in the *Qur'an*, while Muhammad is mentioned only 25 times.

The *Qur'an* teaches that Jesus was:

- a prophet
- born of Mary
- but did not die.

Muslims believe that someone died in Jesus' place, as they think that death would have been a sign of failure.

But the apostle Peter, an eyewitness of Jesus' death, wrote: "For Christ died for sins once for all." 1 PETER 3:18

Islam's holy books

Islam recognizes the Old Testament and the New Testament as authentic revelations from God. But the *Qur'an* is their authoritative book.

For the Christian, there is only one authoritative book and that is the Bible.

We are not free to put another book alongside the Bible as if it had equal authority or, in the case of Islamic belief, more authority.

"I warn everyone who hears the words of the prophecy of this book: If anyone adds anything to them, God will add to him the plagues described in this book." REVELATION 22:18

The Jihad

The word literally means "striving" or "struggle". In practice it is a "holy war" and can involve the promulgation of Islam by force.

Knowing God's will versus knowing God

Islam teaches that God is far removed from humanity. The very best that a Muslim can achieve is to know God's will. He will never be able to know God himself. God may be everywhere but a personal relationship with him is out of the question.

A Muslim theologian once said: "God reveals only his will, not himself. He remains forever hidden."

Jesus said: "I know my sheep and my sheep know me." JOHN 10:14

Jesus also said: "If you really knew me, you would know my Father as well." JOHN 14:7

What about Hinduism?

No founder

Hinduism had no founder. Hinduism began in India about 3,500-4,000 years ago.

Facts and figures

- There are over 800,000,000 Hindus in the world.
- Most Hindus live in southern Asia, especially India, Nepal and Bangladesh.

One God, many gods

There are 33 main deities according to the *Veda*.

The Hindu pantheon has been explained in this way:

"Truth is one; wise men call it by different names." VEDA

Hindus defend accusations of being pantheistic by saying that they believe that the One God has 33 different facets.

Nearly every Hindu home has a shrine that fills a complete room or the corner of a room.

Hindu gods are meant to bring peace and to ward off evil spirits.

The Hindu gods

Among the most important Hindu gods are:

- Brahman, the eternal Trimutri or Three-in-One God
- Brahma, the Creator
- Vishnu, the Preserver
- Shiva, the Destroyer

Other beliefs

- Be submissive towards **Fate** for you are part of Brahman.
- **Karma**. The total of an individual's acts in this life which determine his destiny in his next life on earth.
- **The Law of Karma**. From good must come good and from evil must come evil.
- **Nirvana**. This is the final stage where the soul arrives after it is free from all its rebirths. It is a blissful spiritual state in which the individual is freed from all desire.
- **Yogas**. These are disciplines by means of which the body and emotions can be controlled.
- **Dharma** or the Law of Moral Order must be found and followed by each person who wishes to attain Nirvana.

HINDU SCRIPTURES

1. The Vedas

Veda means wisdom.
The four **Vedas** consist of prayers and hymns.

The **Upanishads** supplement the **Vedas**. There are over one hundred books consisting of stories, conversations and wise sayings.

2. The Great Epics

The **Ramayana** and the **Mahabharata** are the two major epic stories of India. The **Mahabharata** includes the most popular part of the Hindu scriptures – the **Bhagavad Gita** or the "Song of the Blessed Lord".

The importance of this story is that it endorses the Hindu belief of **bhakti** (devotion to a particular god) as a way of achieving salvation. The hero of the story, Arjuna, puts his devotion to Vishnu above his own personal wishes.

Additional information on Hinduism

The sacred cow

Hindus believe that the supreme god lives in all creatures, both humans and animals. From this they reason that all life is sacred.

They think that the cow is the most sacred animal since it gives so much. In return for just eating grass and grain it gives us milk, while leather is made from its hides.

The Hindu reverence for cows is seen in the following verses from the *Atharva Veda* which identify the cow with the rest of the universe:

Worship to thee, springing to life, and worship to thee when born! Worship, O Cow, to thy tail hair, and to thy hooves, and to thy form! The Cow is Heaven, the Cow is Earth, the Cow is Vishnu Lord of Life... He who hath given a Cow unto the Brahmans winneth all the worlds... Both Gods and mortal men depend for life and being upon the Cow... She hath become this universe; all that the sun surveys is she.

The caste system

Hinduism believes that the caste system, a social hierarchy which governs marriages and all other major social actions, should be maintained.

The four major classes within this system are:

1. **The Brahmins** The elite, linked with the priesthood.
2. **The Kshatriyas** The military class and the ruling class.
3. **The Vaisyas** The farmers and businessmen.
4. **The Sudra** The peasants.

At the bottom of the caste system are **The Untouchables** who are reduced to doing the most menial tasks, like burying the dead.

"There is neither Jew nor Greek, slave nor free, male nor female, for you are all one in Christ Jesus." GALATIANS 3:28

The Hindu way of salvation

Hindus believe that salvation is to be achieved in one of the following three ways:

- Through knowledge
- Through devotion – in practice this means obeying a particular deity.
- Through good deeds or keeping ceremonial rituals.

Salvation is attained through an unending cycle of birth, death and rebirth

"All ... are justified freely by his [God's] grace through the redemption that came by Christ Jesus." ROMANS 3:23-24

Praying to an image

Hindus are encouraged to pray to images. This is meant to be a way of finding help in worship.

"The Supreme Personality of Godhead said: those who fix their minds on my personal form and are always engaged in worshiping Me with great and transcendental faith are considered by Me to be most perfect." BHAGAVAD-GITA 12.II

The Bible states: "You shall have no other gods before me. You shall not make for yourself an idol in the form of anything in heaven above or on the earth beneath or in the waters below. You shall not bow down to them or worship them." EXODUS 20:3-5

Reincarnation

As a result of virtuous living a soul can reach a high state through rebirths.

A simple way of understanding the Hindu belief in reincarnation is to think of it as "re-entering the flesh." When a person dies, he or she comes back as another person or as another animal. In this way the soul learns many lessons.

Eventually it can reach a stage called *mukti* when reincarnations cease.

The Bible does not support reincarnation: "... man is destined to die once, and after that to face judgment." HEBREWS 9:27

What about Buddhism?

The origins of Buddhism

Siddhartha Gautama, 563-483 B.C., founded Buddhism. He was born in southern Nepal where his father was a king. His father had been warned by a sage that his son would become an ascetic or a universal monarch, so the prince was never allowed to leave his palace. However he escaped and became a beggar spending his time searching for peace.

The prince who left the palace

The story goes on that Gautama fell into deep meditation under the shade of a fig tree called the *bodhi* or *bo* tree – the tree of wisdom. There he reached the highest degree of God-consciousness known as *Nirvana*. Gautama then spent 40 years teaching the truths he had learned. He became known as the Buddha or Enlightened One.

The four noble truths

Buddha's understanding of the origin of suffering constitute the foundation of Buddhism.

1. **The truth of suffering.** Everyone must suffer.
2. **The cause of suffering.** Suffering is caused by our selfish craving.
3. **Craving can be overcome.** After defeating selfish craving you enter the state of *Nirvana* and all suffering ends.
4. **The way to end craving is an eightfold path.**

KEY WORDS UNRAVELED

Buddha
The word means *The Enlightened One*. It refers to the first Buddha, Gautama, as well as anyone who has reached the state of enlightenment.

Enlightenment
Enlightenment is the realization of the truth of all existence as you pass into the state of *Nirvana*.

Dalai Lama
The world leader of Tibetan Buddhism.

Dharma
A sublime religious truth.

Arhat
An *Arhat* is a holy person who achieves enlightenment through ascetic practices.

Sangha
A *Sangha* is a community of monks or nuns. Buddha's first disciples formed the first *Sangha*.

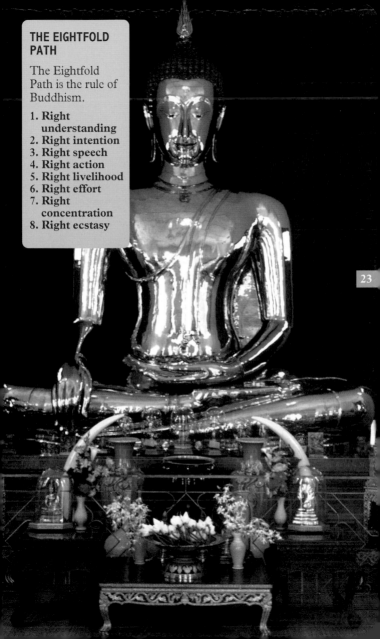

THE EIGHTFOLD PATH

The Eightfold Path is the rule of Buddhism.

1. **Right understanding**
2. **Right intention**
3. **Right speech**
4. **Right action**
5. **Right livelihood**
6. **Right effort**
7. **Right concentration**
8. **Right ecstasy**

Additional information on Buddhism

Where is God in Buddhism?

Buddhism has been called "an atheistic religion" because Buddha rejected all the gods of Hinduism which surrounded him.

In Christianity, to reach the ultimate is to perfectly love, praise and serve God – to be like him and to know him. In Buddhism, to reach the ultimate is to reach Nirvana.

Nirvana

Nirvana is the end of consciousness. It is emptiness.

Zen Buddhism, a Japanese branch of Buddhism, calls this *samori*: a state of bliss in which there is no sense of time and where all thought ceases.

Empty yourself

A man who wanted to become a Zen master asked to be taught Zen. The Zen master did not speak but started to pour a cup of tea for his visitor. He poured the tea into a cup that was already full. The tea overflowed, ran across the table and dripped on to the rice-mat on the floor. The Zen master kept pouring out the tea until the pot was empty. He finally spoke:

"You are like this cup. You are full. How can I pour Zen into you? Empty yourself and come back."

"Be filled with the Spirit."
Ephesians 5:18

No supreme being, no sin, no savior

According to Buddhism the world keeps going through natural power and there is no need for the existence of a personal creator.

Buddhism even denies the existence of a personal God. Buddhism has no savior. The closest it comes to having a savior is the Buddha – the Enlightened One, the Shower-of-the-Way.

There is also no such thing in Buddhism as sin against a supreme being.

Christianity teaches that we do sin against God and so are in need of a Savior.

"She [Mary] will give birth to a son, and you are to give him the name Jesus, because he will save his people from their sins."
Matthew 1:21

Buddhism's Three Jewels

Buddhism's Three Jewels known as *triatna* are: the Buddha, the *Dharma* and the *Sangha*.

The Three Jewels are prayed to when Buddhists meet in their shrines. Gautama is said to have given this invocation to his first missionaries.

> To the Buddha for refuge I go,
> To the Dharma for refuge I go,
> To the Sangha for refuge I go.

"In you, O Lord, I have taken refuge;
... Be my rock of refuge.
... you are my strong refuge."
PSALM 71:1, 3, 7

"Come to me, all you who are weary and burdened, and I will give you rest. Take my yoke upon you and learn from me, for I am gentle and humble in heart, and will find rest for your souls."
MATTHEW 11:28-29

What about Confucianism?

A religion from China

Confucianism has been the leading moral and quasi-religious influence in China for the past two thousand years.

Confucius

Confucius, K'ung-fu-tzu, 551-479 B.C. was born in the state of Lu, northern China. Often hailed as one of world's most influential thinkers, Confucius was more interested in politics and ethics than religion.

Confucian Analects, a collection of his sayings, became the basis of Confucianism alongside the anthologies of the ancient Chinese classics.

Confucius sacrificed to his ancestors and he held ancestor worship to be the highest of virtues.

Ancestor worship was later extended to include the worship of Confucius himself.

The five classics

The five books of the Confucian canon were all written before Confucius lived.

1. The Book of Changes, *I Ching*
2. The Book of History, *Shu Ching*
3. The Book of Poetry, *Shi Ching*
4. The Book of Rites, *Li Chi*
5. The Spring and Autumn Annals, *Ch'un Ch'iu*

I Ching

I Ching is regarded as the most important of the Confucian books and in the West is the most well known. It claims to offer divine counsel to those seeking guidance.

This advice is given in the form of 64 hexagrams (six-line figures). Each hexagram is said to give insight into how an event or phenomenon works.

"It will be advantageous to be firm and correct, and thus there will be free course and success. Let the subject nurture a docility like that of a cow, and there will be good fortune." HEXAGRAM 30 (FIRE)

The five virtues

Confucianism teaches that if these five virtues are followed they lead to the Way of Heaven.

1. **Jen.** *Jen* means benevolence or goodness and emphasizes loyalty and courtesy in the family. Confucious wrote: "Jen is politeness, liberality, good faith, diligence, generosity."

2. **Li.** *Li* is the idea of reverence and respect towards everyone. *Li*, or manners, is the most important virtue after *Jen*. This polite behavior governs inner as well as outer manners. *Li* has 300 major rules and 3,000 minor rules.

3. Yi. *Yi* is duty.

4. Chih. *Chih* is wisdom and includes practical as well as moral knowledge.

5. Hsin. *Hsin* is good faith and is the characteristic of a trustworthy person who keeps his promises.

"The fool says in his heart, 'There is no God.'" PSALM 14:1

"The fear of the Lord is the beginning of wisdom." PSALM 111:10

TAOISM

Taoism, in many ways, is complementary to Confucianism. Taoism traces its origins back to the 6th century B.C., and is based on the teachings of Lao-tzu.

Tao Te Ching, the book attributed to Lao-tzu, teaches that inaction is the best kind of and most creative action. Goal-orientated ways of thinking find no place in Taoism.

Keeping everything simple

"As to dwelling, live near the ground.
As to thinking, hold to that which is simple.
As to conflict, pursue fairness and generosity.
As to government, do not attempt to control.
As to work, do what you like doing.
As to family life, be fully present."
TAO TE CHING

What about Shintoism?

A religion from Japan

Shintoism is the ancient religion of Japan. The form in which it is practiced in Japan today has been influenced by Buddhism and Confucianism.

Characteristics of Shintoism

- It observes customs and traditional rituals. These are more important than religious belief and doctrine.
- Ancestors are revered.
- Popular festivals are celebrated.
- Pilgrimages are made to shrines where it is believed as many as 8,000,000 kami live. Pilgrimages are also made to the top of Mount Fuji.

What Shintoism does *not* have

- Shintoism has no founder.
- Shintoism has no scriptures. It has *Kojiki* and *Nihongi*, two ancient texts from the 8th century A.D. which contain mythological stories and court procedure. It also has the *Yengishiki*, a collection of ritual prayers from the 10th century.
- Shintoism does not have an exclusive form of worship. It can be mingled with Buddhism, as is the case in Japan today.

Amaterasu-O-mikami

Amaterasu-O-mikami is the most exalted of the *kamis*. She is the sun goddess, and the ancestor of the emperors of Japan.

After World War II Emperor Hirohito publically renounced his claim to divinity.

At the shrine

At the Shinto shrine *kami* (which may live in trees, rivers, animals, or in the sun and moon) are worshiped. The worship of ancestors including Japanese heroes and deceased

emperors is still practiced.

The imperial shrine of the sun goddess Amaterasu, at Ise, is the most important Shinto shrine today.

In each shrine one particular *kami* is venerated, with prayers, dancing or by clapping hands.

In the home

Many Japanese homes have a "god-shelf" consisting of a small wooden shrine housing tablets bearing the names of ancestors at which lighted candles and offerings are laid.

Christianity teaches that there is one God, and the way to know him and be at peace with him is through his Son, Jesus.

Key words unraveled

Shinto

The word *Shinto* is not a Japanese word. It comes from China and was introduced when Buddhism first came to Japan. It is derived from two Chinese words *shen* (gods) and *tao* (way), *The Way of the Gods*.

Kami

Kami are divine forces of nature and spirits which are believed to live in shrines. The Japanese nation is "descended" from these *kami*.

"Therefore, since we have been justified through faith, we have peace with God through our Lord Jesus Christ." ROMANS 5:1

What about the New Age Movement?

What is the New Age movement?

The New Age movement has no church, no Bible, no single leader, and no list of members.

It is an umbrella movement embracing a wide range of beliefs and practices.

In part, it grew out of the American counterculture of the 1960s and 70s.

New Age words

The New Age movement is not a religion, but it uses many religious words. It borrows numerous Christian words and often gives the impression of having a Christian "feel" to its ideas.

Characteristic New Age words:

- Holistic
- Holographic
- Synergistic
- Unity
- Oneness
- Harmony
- At-one-ment
- Transformation
- Personal growth
- Human potential
- Awakening
- Networking
- Consciousness
- Energy

It is like a sponge

The New Age movement is like a sponge in the way it collects different ideas from different religions, cultures and philosophies.

It tries to bring these different approaches to life into one unified whole.

Ideas and practices within the New Age movement

- Making the most of one's spiritual dimension.
- Using holistic medicines.
- Belief in reincarnation.
- Belief that events in the world are influenced by the stars.
- Following the general ideas of Eastern religions.
- Practicing nature worship.

Not all fellow travelers within the New Age movement embrace all of these ideas, although many agree with some of them.

The "Aquarian Age"

The term *New Age* refers to the "Aquarian Age", a phrase taken from astrology, which New Age followers believe has dawned.

The New Age movement teaches humanity that we are about to make a great step forward in consciousness and spiritual discovery.

This, it is supposed, will result in peace and enlightenment and reunite humankind with God.

New Agers believe that we must seek the divine that is already within us and so usher in the new millennium as a revived people.

New World Order

Many in the New Age movement are looking forward to a New World Order.

This is variously described as: New Age religion, one-world government or global socialism.

The characteristic of this New World Order is to be self-realized righteousness.

New Agers do not think that humanity is, at present, completely separated from God but that we just need a little more understanding about the true nature of God and reality.

New Agers do not believe that humanity is cut off from God because of sin.

"But your iniquities have separated you from your God." Isaiah 59:2

Additional information on New Age teachings

Shared concerns, but not Christian

Some of the concerns of the New Age movement are shared by Christians, such as care for the environment and criticism of the materialism of the West.

At first sight, some of the New Age ideas seem to coincide with Christian teaching but on further investigation, most New Age ideas are seen to be far from Christian.

Mystical experiences

While New Agers may meditate, this is not praying in the Holy Spirit, through Jesus, to God the Father.

Glory be to man

The New Age movement teaches that humanity is basically good – even divine.

From this it follows that men and women are endowed with divine qualities.

If you are divine, you can then make your own reality. Therefore, if you believe in reincarnation that becomes reality for you. But if your fellow New Ager does not believe in reincarnation that is all right because that is his reality.

The teaching of the Bible declares that, while each person was made in the image of God, this image has become twisted, and everyone is a sinner.

"Therefore, just as sin entered the world through one man, and death through sin, and in this way death came to all men, because all sinned." ROMANS 5:12

Pantheism

New Agers feel that everything is a part of God, that humanity is a part of everything, and so men and women are a part of God. The great Oneness of Being is thought to be "God."

These pantheistic ideas have been taken from eastern mystical religions.

Anything which can be said to have metaphysical roots is labeled as "God."

The New Age "God" is not a moral Being or even the supreme Being. New Agers do not worship God. They think of God as an impersonal and amoral force. More than that, they teach that we are all God.

"This is what the Lord says – your Redeemer, who formed you in the

womb: I am the Lord, who has made all things, who alone stretched out the heavens, who spread out the earth by myself."
ISAIAH 44:24

The New Age view of salvation

In the New Age movement salvation means to be in tune with the divine consciousness. This means being in harmony with reality and with whatever you perceive to be true.

The New Age movement does not have the word "sin" in its vocabulary.

Since the New Age movement does not acknowledge sin or sinfulness, it eliminates the need for a redeemer. Jesus as Savior is not considered to be necessary.

All you need to do, say New Agers, is realize your own divine nature. Salvation consists in thinking in the right way. What you need to be saved from is not sin but ignorance.

If you can understand your own natural godlikeness and goodness and combine this with correct knowledge you are saved.

The teaching of Jesus is that: "No one can enter the kingdom of God unless he is born of water and the Spirit." JOHN 3:5

This spiritual birth is God's gift.

What's the difference between a denomination and a cult?

Religions, denominations, sects and cults

It is helpful to distinguish between religions, denominations and cults.

Sub-divisions

Each world religion, including Christianity, is divided into branches. The sub-divisions within the Christian faith are known as Churches: the Roman Catholic Church, the Protestant Church and the Eastern Orthodox Church. Protestantism has its own sub-divisions, and these are known as denominations such as the Baptists, the Methodists and the Lutherans.

The Christian faith is summed up in the Nicene Creed, formulated in the Council of Nicea, in A.D. 325, when Arianism was rejected.

The Nicene Creed

We believe in one God,
the Father, the Almighty,
maker of heaven and earth,
of all that is, seen and unseen.

We believe in one Lord, Jesus Christ,
the only Son of God,
eternally begotten of the Father,
God from God, Light from Light,
true God from true God,
begotten, not made,
of one Being with the Father.
Through him all things were made.
For us and for our salvation
he came down from heaven:
by the power of the Holy Spirit
he became incarnate from the Virgin
    Mary,
and was made man.
For our sake he was crucified under
    Pontius Pilate;
he suffered death and was buried.
On the third day he rose again
in accordance with the Scriptures;
he ascended into heaven
and is seated at the right hand of
    the Father.

SECTS AND CULTS

Sects are groups of people who have broken away from generally accepted orthodox Christianity. They have at least one major disagreement (heresy) in their teaching which normally centers around the deity of Jesus and the place of the Bible as a rule of faith.

A cult is a religious group which is usually considered to be extreme and heretical by members of mainstream Christianity. Members of certain small cults often live in unconventional ways under the grip of an authoritarian, charismatic leader.

1. Non-Christian faiths

RELIGION	% OF WORLD POP	TOTAL ADHERENTS IN MILLIONS	GROWTH RATE
Muslim	19.6	1,035	2.9%
Non-religious	18.3	969	4.5%
Hindu	13.5	716	2%
Buddhist/Eastern religions	11.6	613	2.1%
Chinese folk religion (Taoism, Confucianism)	2.7	144	0.2%
Sikh	0.3	17.2	2.3%
Jews	0.25	13.4	1.3%
Baha'i	0.1	5	5.5%
Other	0.8	48	

2. Christianity

Protestant	10.3	543	3.3%
Roman Catholic	16.8	792	1.3%
Other Catholic	0.2	9.7	0.8%
Orthodox	4.1	215	3.3%

3. Sects

Total	1.4	74	6.9%
Christian Scientists	0.02	1	
Mormons	0.2	9	
Jehovah's Witnesses	0.1	5	

He will come again in glory to judge the living and the dead, and his kingdom will have no end.

We believe in the Holy Spirit, the Lord, the giver of life, who proceeds from the Father and the Son.
With the Father and the Son he is worshiped and glorified.
He has spoken through the Prophets.
We believe in one holy catholic and apostolic Church.

We acknowledge one baptism for the forgiveness of sins.
We look for the resurrection of the dead,
and the life of the world to come. Amen.

Who is growing, who is shrinking?

- Christianity is growing at a slower rate than the increase of the world population.
- The fastest growing world religion is Islam.

What about Roman Catholicism?

The Roman Catholic claim

Roman Catholicism maintains that the life of the Church, meaning the community of all those who believe in Jesus Christ, is truly united with the risen life of Jesus, present here and now; and that this union with Jesus, which offers a share in his work of teaching and making available the grace of the Holy Spirit, is most fully expressed in Roman Catholicism.

Apostolic succession

The activity of teaching and sanctifying, shared in some measure by all Christians, is rooted in the unique exercise of this activity by the bishops. Their own unity is centered on the bishop of Rome, called the Pope, and they are said to have received their role in a direct historical line tracing back to the twelve apostles. This idea that the authority of the bishops derives from Jesus through the apostles is known as the

Facts and figures
- There are nearly 250 million more Roman Catholics than Protestants.
- There are nearly four times as many Roman Catholics as there are members of the Eastern Orthodox Church.

doctrine of apostolic succession. Catholics refer to the revealed teaching which Jesus gave to his Church as Tradition. Even though the word "infallible" is used, in the first instance, to refer to the faith of the Church, meaning that the Church's faith in Jesus will never fail, it is used in a special way to speak of the certainty Christians can have that when the Pope, as the successor to the apostle Peter, speaks *ex cathedra* ("from the chair") – referring to his role as principal teacher in the Church – he is accurately passing on the teaching first given to the Church by Jesus.

KEYS WORDS UNRAVELED

Catholic
The term *Catholic* means universal.

Roman Catholic
The term *Roman Catholic* first came into use in Britain in the seventeenth century but is now in common use among English-speaking people.

TWO DEEP DIVISIONS

As a result of two great divisions a distinctly "Roman Catholic" tradition developed.

1. The "Great Schism"
In 1054 the Eastern Church, (Byzantine Church) split from the Western, Roman Church.

2. The Reformation
Western Christendom was further split in the sixteenth-century by the Protestant Reformation. The decrees issued by the Council of Trent, 1545-63, affirmed many of the Roman Catholic doctrines and attacked the biblical teaching of the Protestants

Tradition and the Bible
Roman Catholics believe that the Bible is authoritative in matters of Christian doctrine and practice. However, they also regard the teaching tradition of the Roman Catholic Church as having equal authority.

"... the Church, to whom the transmission and interpretation of Revelation is entrusted, 'does not derive her certainty about all revealed truths from the holy Scriptures alone. Both Scripture and Tradition must be accepted and honored with equal sentiments of devotion and reverence'."

CATECHISM OF THE CATHOLIC CHURCH, PAR. 82

Additional information on Roman Catholicism

Key doctrines
There are numerous teachings which Roman Catholics believe.

St Peter's Basilica, Rome

ROMAN CATHOLIC PRACTICES

1. Communion of Saints

Roman Catholics are taught that the Church is a community of all the faithful, living and dead, who form as it were a single body, having Christ as its head and source of life.

2. Offering of masses and prayers for those who suffer in "purgatory"

Roman Catholics maintain that believers whose growth in Christ has, at death, still not attained to the full maturity required for final unity with the Father enter a stage of purification known as purgatory. The Catholic *Catechism* states, "All who die in God's grace and friendship, but still imperfectly purified, are indeed assured of their eternal salvation; but after death they undergo purification, so as to achieve the holiness necessary to enter the joy of heaven...." CATECHISM 1030–31

3. Beliefs about Mary, Jesus' mother

In view of her decision whereby she would consent to be the mother of the Messiah, Mary, from the moment of her conception, was filled with Christ's grace, was redeemed from original sin, and so was made free to give her entire self unreservedly to the Father's will. This is called the teaching of the Immaculate Conception and was formally declared a dogma of faith in 1854.

- She is said to have been perfectly sinless throughout her life.
- She is said to be always a virgin.

4. The sacrifice of the Mass

Roman Catholics believe that in the sacrament of the Lord's Supper, Jesus, through the action of the priest, makes his life and death present for the faithful, so that they may join themselves to the sacrifice he made once and for all on Calvary, the sacrifice which alone suffices for salvation. This sacrament is considered to be the Church's greatest prayer, and it is offered on behalf of all, including the dead, who have not yet entered the Father's glory. It is also believed that by the power of the Holy Spirit, the bread and wine of the sacrament are made more than signs of Jesus' presence, and actually become his risen body and blood.

5. Salvation

Roman Catholics teach that the Holy Spirit offers the grace of salvation to everyone, in every time, through the merits of Jesus Christ, united with his Church.

The Second Vatican Council's Decree on Ecumenism (1.3) states: "For it is through Christ's Catholic Church alone, which is the universal help toward salvation, that the fullness of the means of salvation can be obtained."

What about Protestantism?

Protestants and the Reformation

The three Christian traditions are Roman Catholic, Orthodox and Protestant. "Protestant" is a generic title given to those who split in "protest" with the Roman Catholic Church at the time of the Reformation.

Two of the leading features of Protestantism are:

1. Its emphasis on the authority of the Bible over the authority of church traditions.
2. Its rejection of any suggestion of a priestly hierarchy.

The Reformation resulted in a rediscovery of the Bible. The Bible now became available to the lay person, not just the clergy.

The Protestant watchword

The emphases of Reformation thought can be summarized as follows:
- by faith *alone*,
- by Scripture *alone*,
- by grace *alone*,
- by Christ *alone*,
- for God's glory *alone*.

Sola scriptura

One of the watchwords of the Reformation was *sola scriptura* (Scripture alone).

The conscience of a Biblical Protestant like Luther or Calvin was bound by the Bible alone.

The Reformers believed that the Scriptures of the Old and New Testaments were the Word of God – the only infallible rule for faith and life.

Today, evangelicals are heirs of reformation beliefs and their emphasis on the teachings of the Bible.

Martin Luther, 1483-1546

Since the fifteenth-century, the Roman Catholic Church had taught that indulgences could be bought on behalf of souls in purgatory as well as for the living. An indulgence was the remission of temporal punishment still due for a sin that had been sacramentally absolved. It was believed that forgiveness of one's sins could be bought in this way.

Luther spoke out against the practice of granting indulgences as this was opposed to the basic Bible teaching about God's free and complete forgiveness.

Luther nailed his **95 Theses** to the church door in Wittenberg in protest.

Luther's public debates with John Eck, the leading Roman Catholic theologian, his translation of the Bible into straightforward German, and his lectures on the Psalms, Romans, Galatians and Hebrews paved the way for the Reformation in Germany and beyond.

John Calvin, 1509-1564

Calvin was born in France, but exiled to Geneva in Switzerland where he became the Reformation's greatest Bible teacher.

Calvin's *Institutes of the Christian Religion* remain one of *the* classic statements of Protestantism.

Calvin's commentaries on nearly every book of the Bible are still studied by Christians today.

Calvin's teaching about God's sovereignty greatly influenced many pastors and preachers, including Richard Baxter, John Bunyan, George Whitefield, Jonathan Edwards and Charles Spurgeon.

What about the Baptists, Brethren, Congregationalists, Episcopalians and Anglicans, Lutherans, Methodists, Presbyterians and Reformed churches?

Protestants today

One of the characteristics of Protestants is the numerous denominations they are split up into.

Baptists

One of the characteristic beliefs of Baptists is that they believe in believer's baptism, following a person's conversion, and are opposed to the baptism of babies.

William Carey (1761-1834), an English Baptist, was a pioneer missionary in India where he translated the Bible, planted churches and provided medical care. His life reflects the strong missionary concern of Baptists.

The evangelist, Billy Graham, is one of the most well-known Baptists of the twentieth-century.

The Brethren

The distinctive characteristic of the Brethren is that the gifts and ministry of the church are given to all believers. Their simple worship services and communion services are led by different members of their own congregations and many have no full-time pastors. In the U.S. there are several denominations, of which the largest is the Church of the Brethren.

Congregationalists

Separatist Puritans broke away from the Anglican Church in 1581, called themselves Brownists, and formed an independent congregation at Norwich, Norfolk, England. This marked the beginning of the English Independent or Congregationalist movement. In Congregationalist churches each congregation governs itself and does not submit to the oversight of a hierarchy of bishops.

Jonathan Edwards (1703-1758), the preacher during the time of the Great Awakening, was one of the best-known Congregationalists.

Episcopalians and Anglicans

The Anglican Church is a worldwide body of churches that are in communion with the Church of England. Member churches include the Protestant Episcopal Church in America (Episcopalians).

Their distinctive pattern of worship is traditionally based on *The Book of Common Prayer*.

They accept the threefold pattern of ministry of bishops, presbyters (priests) and deacons.

Methodists

John Wesley led a group of students at Oxford University in Bible study, prayer and social concern. This group was referred to as the "Holy Club." They became known as "Methodists" as they were so methodical in everything they did, especially in the organization of the societies which nurtured Christian growth.

When some Anglican ministers were barred from preaching their evangelical message in Anglican churches in England they adopted Whitefield's novel practice of preaching in the open air. John Wesley split from Anglicans and formed what we now know as the Methodist Church.

Presbyterian and Reformed churches

Presbyterianism is the main branch of the Reformed churches and embodies many of the principles of Calvinism.

In 1557 John Knox founded a Presbyterian church in Scotland.

The first Presbyterian church in America appeared in 1626 after the Dutch East India Company founded a colony on the Hudson River and became well known for its biblical preaching. R.C. Sproul is a contemporary notable Presbyterian preacher.

Lutherans

Lutherans trace their history back to the time of the New Testament and confess the biblical doctrines summarized in the Apostles' Creed.

Lutheranism as a movement within the Christian Church is traditionally dated as beginning on October 31, 1517, the day the Martin Luther posted the 95 *theses* to the door of the castle church in Wittenberg. These 95 theses highlighted the abuses in the Church of Luther's day.

There are more than 80 million baptized Lutherans in the world.

Nearly 9 million Lutherans live in North America.

What about the Eastern Orthodox Church?

When did they start?

The Orthodox or Eastern Orthodox or Orthodox Eastern Church came into existence in eastern Europe and south-west Asia after it split with the Western Church.

The Orthodox Church traces its origins back to the times of Jesus' apostles who preached in the Greek-speaking communities of Corinth, Antioch and Ephesus.

The Great Schism

The split between East and West, which had already begun in the 5th century, became a reality in 1045 when Pope Leo IX condemned the patriarch of Constantinople.

The Orthodox Church accepted the decrees of the first seven ecumenical councils, held between A.D. 325 and 787. These decrees and the teaching of the early Fathers are still important in the Orthodox Church.

The Orthodox Church rejects the jurisdiction of the Pope and waits for the bishop of Rome "to admit his error".

The Orthodox Church and Roman Catholics regard each other as schismatic.

What's different in the Orthodox Church?

- Children are allowed to receive the bread and wine at the Lord's Supper.
- The Orthodox liturgy (services used for public worship) are based on the liturgies of St John Chrysostom and St Basil.
- Orthodox services are sung rather than said.
- Orthodox priests are allowed to marry before they are ordained.
- The orthodox churches are self-governing, but loosely held together in a bond of unity.

KEY WORDS UNRAVELED

Icon
An *icon*, often displayed in Orthodox churches, is a religious picture painted in oil on a small wooden panel.

Patriarch
A *patriarch* is the head of one of the Eastern Orthodox churches.

WHERE THE ORTHODOX CHURCH FITS IN

Jesus and the early church

THE GREAT SCHISM

Eastern Orthodox
Greek, Russian, Armenian

Western Catholic

THE REFORMATION

Roman Catholic

Protestant
Protestant denominations

Decorated churches

The decorations inside an Orthodox church give a background of beauty in which their worship services are set. There is often:

- gilding
- decorated screens
- carved ornamentations
- incense
- icons.

Prayer of John Chrysostom, 347-407, bishop of Constantinople

"Almighty God, who has given us grace at this time with one accord to make our common supplications to you; and has promised that when two or three are gathered together in your name you will grant their requests: fulfil now, O Lord, the desires and petitions of your servants, as may be most expedient for them; granting us in this world knowledge of your truth, and in the world to come life everlasting."

What about Mormonism?

Their name
The official name of the Mormon Church is: The Church of Jesus Christ of Latter-day Saints (LDS).

Joseph Smith
The Mormons teach that the true church ceased to exist until it was restored by Joseph Smith on April 6, 1830.

Two golden plates
Joseph Smith claims that an angel called Moroni told him about a box hidden in the Hill Cumorah near Palmyra. After finding the box Smith is supposed to have taken three years to translate the writing on the two golden plates found there. Smith published his translation as *The Book of Mormon* in 1830.

The angel then took these plates away so no one else has ever seen them.

On April 6, 1830 in Fayette, New York, the church began with six members. Joseph Smith became their "seer, a translator, a prophet, an apostle of Jesus Christ".

The influence of the Mormons
• There are nearly nine million Mormons in the world – over half of whom live in America.

Mormons and revelation

Mormons stress the importance of revelation.

The books the Mormons use to compile their beliefs are:
- The Bible
- *The Book of Mormon*
- *Doctrine and Covenants*, (revelations given to Joseph Smith)
- *The Pearl of Great Price* (sayings attributed to Moses and Abraham)

The zeal of the Mormons

- The Mormons do not drink alcohol, tea or coffee, or smoke.
- More people visit the Salt Lake Temple Square each year than visit the Grand Canyon or the Statue of Liberty.
- The Mormons have compiled a list of more than two billion (2,000,000,000) people who have died and store this record in a vault in a granite mountain near Salt Lake City. They have now made this list available on the Internet.
- There are 46,000 Mormon missionaries active throughout the world. They aim to have 100,000 missionaries by the year 2000.
- Mormons claim that for every Mormon who leaves the Mormon Church for a Christian Church forty people leave Christian Churches and become Mormons. The Mormons train their members to win others to the Mormon Church.

Additional information on Mormonism

How do Mormon teachings differ from those in the Bible?

1 Belief about humanity

Mormons teach that men and women can become gods and goddesses and that those who achieve this godhood will be worshiped by others.

"This is what the Lord says – Israel's King and Redeemer, the Lord Almighty: I am the first and I am the last; apart from me there is no God." ISAIAH 44:6

2 Belief about God the Father

The Mormons teach that God the Father was once a man who later become a God. They say that he still has a physical body made of flesh and bone. "The Father has a body of flesh and bones as tangible as man's. ... As man is, God once was; as God is, man may be." DOCTRINE AND COVENANTS

"Before the mountains were born or you brought forth the earth and the world, from everlasting to everlasting you are God." PSALM 90:2

3 Belief about God the Son

Mormons teach that Jesus Christ is our elder brother and that he, himself, progressed to godhood.

Mormons teach that Jesus Christ was born as a result of God the Father having sexual intercourse with Mary. "When the Virgin Mary conceived the Child Jesus ... He was not begotten by the Holy Ghost. And who is his Father? He is the first of the human family." JOURNAL OF DISCOURSES

"In the beginning was the Word, and the Word was with God, and the Word was God. ... The Word became flesh and made his dwelling among us." John 1:1, 14

Mormons teach that Jesus married and was polygamous. "We say it was Jesus Christ who was married at Cana of Galilee." JOURNAL OF DISCOURSES

4 Belief about God the Holy Spirit

The Book of Mormon teaches that the Holy Spirit is a spirit in the form of a man.

5 Baptism on behalf of the dead

The Mormons teach salvation for the dead by proxy water baptism.

Mormons baptize each other in place of non-Mormons who are now dead. They believe that in the afterlife, the newly baptized person will enter into a higher level of Mormon heaven. They derive this from 1 Corinthians 15:29: "Now if there is no resurrection, what will those do who are baptized for the dead? If the dead are not raised at all, why are people baptized for them?"

But Paul is not saying that he practiced baptism for the dead. He simply mentions this irregular type of baptism but nowhere suggests that Christians should follow the practice.

What about Jehovah's Witnesses?

Charles Taze Russell

The Jehovah's Witnesses were founded by Charles Taze Russell of Pennsylvania in the 1870's.

Until 1931 members of this movement were called Russellites.

After Russell's death in 1916 Joseph Franklin Rutherford became their president.

At one of Rutherford's conventions held on October 9 1931 the present name of Jehovah's Witnesses was adopted. They based the name on the words in Isaiah 43:10: "'You are my witnesses,' declares the Lord."

The *New World* Bible

After Rutherford died in 1942, Nathan Homer Knorr took over the presidency and published the *New World*: their own version of the Bible, from which Jehovah's Witnesses derive most of their distinctive teaching.

From 100,000 towards 9,000,000

Under Knorr's leadership the movement's membership rose from just over 100,000 to two and a quarter million.

After Knorr died in 1977 he was replaced by Frederick Franz, until he died in 1992, aged 99. Milton G. Henschel then took over the leadership.

The four and a half million members of the Jehovah's Witnesses of 1992 are now over eight million.

Watchtower magazine

Charles Russell founded the *Herald of the Morning* in 1879 which developed into today's *Watchtower* magazine.

From an initial monthly print run of 4,000 copies it now prints 18 million copies every month in more than 100 languages. It has become the most influential way of perpetuating the Jehovah's Witness teachings.

SEVEN STEPS that Jehovah's Witnesses use to win others to their faith

1. Put Jehovah's Witness literature into the hands of a prospective convert.
2. Revisit this person to establish further personal contact.
3. Introduce the person to the study of Jehovah's Witness books.
4. Encourage the person to attend teaching meetings at a kingdom hall.
5. Encourage the person to attend services at a kingdom hall.
6. Encourage the person to become active in "publishing" – giving out Jehovah's Witness tracts.
7. Encourage the person to become baptized by immersion in a kingdom hall.

Some unusual practices followed by the Jehovah's Witnesses

1. Blood transfusions are refused.
2. The cross should not be used as a symbol.
3. They refuse to vote in political elections, salute the flag or sing the Star Spangled Banner.
4. They do not celebrate Christmas or birthdays.
5. They refuse to serve in the armed forces.

Enthusiastic witnessing

All Jehovah's Witnesses are strongly encouraged to be very active in proselytizing for the movement.

Most Jehovah's Witnesses are expected to spend five hours a week at training sessions held in a kingdom hall, as well as door to door visiting in a selected area. Often, a Jehovah's Witness will devote up to 100 hours a month to the movement.

Additional information on the Jehovah's Witnesses

Jehovah's Witnesses' attitudes toward basic Christian beliefs

ORTHODOX CHRISTIAN BELIEF	JEHOVAH'S WITNESS ATTITUDE
The Trinity	Denied
Personality of the Holy Spirit	Denied
Two natures of Christ, God and human	Denied
Forgiveness of sins through faith in Christ	Denied
Christ's bodily resurrection	Denied
Second coming of Jesus	Distorted
Infallibility of the Bible	Distorted
Final judgment	Distorted
Eternal life in heaven	Distorted

Jehovah's Witnesses also teach that there is no salvation outside their own ranks.

Setting a date for the second coming of Jesus

Much of the teaching of the Jehovah's Witnesses revolves around their view of the imminent second coming of Jesus.

They have often set a date when Jesus would return. 1874, 1914, 1925 and 1975 are four of the dates which were predicted for Jesus' return.

But Jesus said, "No one knows about that day or hour, not even the angels in heaven, nor the Son, but only the Father." MATTHEW 24:36

What Jehovah's Witnesses believe about Jesus

The most serious heresies held by Jehovah's Witnesses concern their beliefs about Jesus.
- They believe that Jesus was a perfect man.
- They do not believe that he is God. They admit that he is "a god" but not "the God."
- They teach that Jesus "was and is and always will be beneath Jehovah" and that "Christ and God are not coequal".
- They deny that Jesus' resurrection was a bodily resurrection.

SOME BIBLE TEACHINGS that refute the teaching of the Jehovah's Witnesses

Jehovah's Witnesses are usually better drilled about their beliefs than Christians are.

1. Jesus was God

"I and the Father are one." JOHN 10:30
See also: John 1:1; 14:10; 17:5; Acts 2:36; 1 John 5:20. Reflect on the attributes of Christ which show that he is God.

- Jesus Christ knows all things: see John 1:48; 2:25; 6:64; 14:30.
- Jesus is all-powerful: see Matthew 28:18; Mark 4:39; Hebrews 1:3
- Jesus is sinless: see John 8:46
- Jesus is eternal: see John 8:58
- Jesus never changes: see Hebrews 13:8
  As only God possesses these attributes, Christ must be God.

2. Jesus was both man and God

Colossians 2:9 is a clear statement of Jesus' divinity and humanity:

"For in Christ all the fullness of the Deity lives in bodily form."

See also John 1:1; Romans 1:3-4; 9:5; Galatians 4:4; Luke 2:7.

3. Jesus rose from the dead

The Bible clearly teaches that Jesus rose in bodily form from the dead. See John 20:19-29; John 2:20-21

What about Christian Scientism?

Different names
Christian Scientism is known by various names:
- Christian Science Church
- The Church of Christ Science
- The First Church of Christ, Scientist

Facts and figures
- It was founded in 1875, in Massachusetts, by Mary Baker Eddy.
- Worldwide, it has 1 million members, 3,000 churches, in 56 countries, with 700,000 members in the USA.

Distinctive teaching
Although a distinctive part of Christian Science is the healing of disease by spiritual means alone, its main purpose is universal salvation from every phase of evil – including sin and death.

Mary Baker Eddy's achievements
Mary Baker Eddy, 1821-1910, is still revered by her followers as:

• An active healer
She claimed to heal people who had incurable ailments and established a widely practiced system of prayer-based healing.

• A pioneer thinker
She is supposed to have opened new doors in theology, medicine, and science.

PUBLICATIONS
- *Christian Science Monitor*
  This is its influential daily newspaper, with a circulation of more than 100,000 copies. It has won the Pulitzer Prize for newspaper publishing.
- Their two magazines are *Christian Science Sentinel*, and *Journal*.

Key books
- Alongside the Bible are set the books of Mary Baker Eddy: *Science and Health*, with *Key to the Scriptures*.

Miscellaneous Writings
- *Manual of the Mother Church*
- In 1992, the Women's National Book Association named *Science and Health* as one of 75 books by women "whose words have changed the world."

• A reformer

She founded a church, teaching college, publishing company and a newspaper.

In 1995, she was elected to the National Women's Hall of Fame as the only American woman to found a worldwide religion.

Mary Baker Eddy's "discovery"

Eddy suffered much ill health during her childhood and adult life. Then, in 1866, when she was 46 years old as she read about Jesus healing the paralysed man in Matthew 9:2-8, she claims that she was healed of a serious injury.

As a result of her "glimpse of the great fact" that life is in and of God, which she called her great discovery, Mary Baker Eddy went on to found the Science of Christianity which she named Christian Science.

After this she claims to have healed many people herself. Eddy taught her students that through prayer they could cure sickness.

In 1892 Eddy reorganized her Boston church and renamed it The First Church of Christ, Scientist, or The Mother Church.

Additional information on Christian Scientism

The Church of Christ Science
Christian Science claims to be the science of healing but on close inspection it becomes clear that it is:
- anti-Christian,
- anti-science,
- anti-healing,
- not a church.

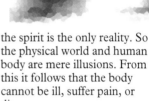

It is anti-science
Christian Science does not believe in the most basic scientific thought, that the universe is physical and is subject to natural laws.

It teaches that the material world does not exist and that the spirit is the only reality. So the physical world and human body are mere illusions. From this it follows that the body cannot be ill, suffer pain, or die.

HERETICAL TEACHING

Christian Scientism teaches a heretical form of Christianity.

God
God is an impersonal Principle of life, truth, love, intelligence, and spirit. He is more like a Hindu god than the Christian God. Christian Scientism teaches that God is not a divine person, but the divine principle of all that exists.

Jesus Christ
- Jesus Christ is not God. He was merely a man who displayed the Christ idea.
- Jesus did not suffer and could not suffer for sins.
- Jesus did not die on the cross, and he did not rise physically.
- Jesus will not literally come back.
- The Virgin Birth was a spiritual idea.

The Holy Spirit
Christian Science teaches that the Holy Spirit is an impersonal power.

Salvation
Salvation comes by recognizing that you are as much a Son of God as Jesus is. There is no sin to be saved from. You are reincarnated until you become perfect.

Christian Scientism is not a Church

Christian Science "services", which are lectures in halls, can appear to be Christian, because the Bible is read.

But there are no sermons, only selected readings from Mary Baker Eddy's books, especially *Science and Health*, with *Key to the Scriptures*, which she claimed was co-authored by God.

In 1895, Eddy established the *Bible* and *Science and Health* as "Pastor" of the Christian Science Churches.

It is anti-healing

Christian Scientists believe that healing comes from realizing one cannot be sick or hurt.

- They go to "practitioners".
- They do not go to doctors or take drugs and vitamins.
- They are against immunization.
- Mary Baker Eddy never managed to produce convincing medical evidence about any of her claimed healings.

The Bible "plus"

"Your dual and impersonal pastor, the Bible, and Science and Health with Key to the Scriptures, is with you; and the Life these give, the Truth they illustrate, the Love they demonstrate, is the great Shepherd that feedeth my flock, and leadeth them 'beside the still waters.'"
MARY BAKER EDDY

A warning from the book of Revelation

"I warn everyone who hears the words of the prophecy of this book: If anyone adds anything to them, God will add to him the plagues described in this book."
REVELATION 22:18

What about Unitarian Universalists?

The Unitarian Church
The first church having the Unitarian faith was organized in Poland by Faustus Socinus in 1587.

The first organized Unitarian movement was started in England by Theophilus Lindsey in 1774.

Unitarians have been especially influential in New England churches since the middle of the 18th century.

The Universalists
The Universalists were first established in the United States in 1779 by a former English Methodist, John Murray.

Unitarian Universalists

Their appeal
Unitarian Universalists say they appeal to people who are looking for:
• a religious home
• open dialogue on questions of faith
• a religious community that affirms spiritual exploration as a way of truth
• a church that acts locally on issues such as: women's rights, racial justice, homelessness, and gay and lesbian rights.

Their beliefs
Unitarian Universalists claim to be a liberal religion in the Jewish and Christian traditions. They believe:
• that personal experience, reason and conscience are the final authorities in religion. They say that religious authority lies not in a book or a great leader or institution but in each individual person.
• that it is never necessary to be bound by a statement of belief.

Unitarian-Universalist association

In 1961 the Unitarian Church merged with the Universalist Church to form the Unitarian Universalist Association (UUA).

Famous Unitarians and Universalists

Famous Unitarians and Universalists include John Adams, Clara Barton, Oliver Wendell Holmes, Louisa May Alcott, Ralph Waldo Emerson and Susan B. Anthony.

Self-governing

Each local congregation, (called a church, society or fellowship) is self-governing and adopts its own bylaws, elects its own officers and approves its own budget.

Fighting against oppression

Since its early work helping victims of Nazi oppression, the UUA has been helping people around the world to help themselves by means of its advocacy programs.

Distinctive doctrines

The chief Unitarian doctrine is the unity or oneness of God. This involves rejecting the doctrine of the Trinity. Universalism's characteristic teaching is the denial of everlasting punishment for unbelievers and the belief that everyone will eventually be saved.

They never ask their members to subscribe to a creed. They delight in being a religion without a creed.

- that religious wisdom is always changing and that human understanding about the world can never be final.
- they should be a positive moral force in the world. They believe that ethical living is the supreme witness of religion.

Additional information on Unitarianism

Its doctrine

Some of the central teachings of Unitarians and Universalists are anti-Christian:
- they deny the Trinity,
- they deny the deity of Jesus,
- they teach universal complete salvation of all living beings.

Socinianism

Unitarians embrace a teaching called Socinianism.

Socinianism derives its name from a doctrine developed in 1550 by the Italian brothers Laelius and Faustus Socinus. They
- denied the Trinity
- taught that Jesus is not God
- taught that the atonement of Jesus is invalid
- taught that salvation is only by works.

Universalism

Universalism has its roots in the eighteenth-century enlightenment and its emphasis on anti-supernaturalism. It teaches that all living beings attain complete salvation.

Traditional Christian teaching about the Trinity

Orthodox, Bible-based Christian teaching about the Trinity was well summarized by the Missouri Synod.

"On the basis of the Holy Scriptures we teach the sublime article of the Holy Trinity; that is, we teach that the one true God, DEUTERONOMY 6:4; 1 CORINTHIANS. 8:4, is the Father and the Son and the Holy Ghost, three distinct persons, but of one and the same divine essence,

equal in power,
equal in eternity,
equal in majesty,

because each person possesses the one divine essence entire, COLOSSIANS 2:9, MATTHEW 28:19.

We hold that all teachers and communions that deny the doctrine of the Holy Trinity are outside the pale of the Christian Church.

The Triune God is the God who is gracious to man, JOHN 3:16-18, 1 CORINTHIANS 12:3. Since the Fall, no man can believe in the fatherhood of God except he believe in the eternal Son of God, who became man and reconciled us to God by His vicarious satisfaction, 1 JOHN 2:23; JOHN 14:6.

Hence we warn against Unitarianism, which in our country has to a great extent infiltrated the sects and is being spread particularly also through the influence of the lodges."

Universalism

The teaching of the Bible is opposed to the idea that God will eventually save everyone. It teaches the certainty of a future judgment and condemnation of some people. If God was going to save everyone judgment would be unnecessary.

"... man is destined to die once, and after that to face judgment." HEBREWS 9:27

The teachings of the Bible never hint of a "second chance" being given to people.

Don't all religions lead to God?

Isn't it enough to be religious?

When the missionary Paul arrived in Athens he soon saw that very religious people lived there.

"Paul then stood up in the meeting of the Areopagus and said: 'Men of Athens! I see that in every way that you are very religious.'" ACTS 17:22

So, did Paul say to himself: "These are very religious people, there's no need to preach to them about Jesus."?

No! Paul continued:

"'For as I walked around and looked carefully at your objects of worship, I even found an altar with this inscription: TO AN UNKNOWN GOD. Now what you worship as something unknown I am going to proclaim to you.'" ACTS 17:23

Can truth contradict itself?

It is often claimed that all religions are different paths to the same place.

There is a fallacy in such reasoning. If all religions are different paths to the same place how is it that the paths contradict each other? How can this be if truth cannot contradict itself?

- **Buddhism** is pantheistic and does not believe in a personal God.
- **Islam** maintains says that Jesus was only a prophet and that he was not the only way to God.
- **Christianity** teaches that there is a personal God and that the only way to God is through Jesus.

If truth is truth, these three religions cannot all be right.

"Can't I trust my feelings?"

Many people simply follow the religion which appeals to them and which feels right. If one could arrive at a correct believe in God by one's feelings there would be no need for the Bible.

The Bible stresses that the heart is deceitful and untrustworthy.

"The heart is deceitful above all things and beyond cure. Who can understand it?" JEREMIAH 17:9

Is there anything positive in non-Christian religion?

As far as salvation is concerned, Christianity teaches that Jesus is the only way to God.

But to say this is not to deny that flashes of God's brilliance, love, and grace may be seen in many unexpected places.

"Your Father in heaven ... causes his sun to rise on the evil and the good, and sends rain on the righteous and the unrighteous." MATTHEW 5:45

Leading people from where they are to Jesus

Cornelius, a non-Jew, and a centurion "in what was known as the Italian Regiment" (Acts 10:1) sent one of his men to ask Peter to visit him and explain the gospel to him.

When Peter arrived, he did not condemn Cornelius for any of his short-comings and faulty beliefs.

Instead, he told the Roman soldier and his family about Jesus.

Peter said, "I now realize how true it is that God does not show favoritism but accepts men from every nation who fear him and do what is right. You know the message God sent to the people of Israel, telling the good news of peace through Jesus Christ, who is Lord of all." ACTS 10:34-36

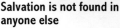

Is Jesus the only way to God?

Jesus claimed to be God

"I and the Father are one."
JOHN 10:30

Jesus said he was the only way to God

"Jesus answered [Thomas],
'I am the way
and the truth
and the life.
No one comes to the Father except through me.
If you really knew me, you would know my Father as well."
JOHN 14:6

Salvation is not found in anyone else

After Jesus' ascension the followers of Jesus set about preaching the good news that he, and he alone, was the Savior of the world.

"The priests and the captain of the temple guard and the Sadducees came up to Peter and John while they were speaking to the people. They were greatly disturbed because the apostles were teaching the people and proclaiming in Jesus the resurrection of the dead. They seized Peter and John, and because it was evening, they put them in jail." ACTS 4:1-3

"The next day ... Peter, filled with the Holy Spirit, said to them ...
ACTS 4:5, 8

'Salvation is found in no one else, for there is no other name under heaven given to men by which we must be saved.'" ACTS 4:12

Knowing God

"We know God only through Jesus Christ." PASCAL